By the Same Author

Etre Soi-même. Genève: Poésie Vivante, 1967.
Rule of Life. Geneva: Poésie Vivante, 1969.
Lightning. New York: Vantage Press 1970.
Reflections/Réflexions. Bloomington, IN: AuthorHouse, 2004.
  (Various texts in English, french, and Arabic)
A Speech to the Arab Nation. The East/theWest/the Arabs: Yes-
  terday, Today and Tomorrow, and Related Writings. Blooming-
  ton, IN: AuthorHouse, 2007. (Text only in Arabic)
To Be Oneself: The Tragicomedy of an Unfinished Life History.
Bloomington, IN: AuthorHouse, 2008.

Language teaching materials

Arabic Language Course, Part One/Cours de langue arabe,
  1ère partie. 2nd ed. Genève: Poésie Vivante, 1979.
Arabic Language Course, Part Two/Cours de langue arabe,
  2ème partie. Geneva: The Author, 1979.
Arabic Grammar/Grammaire arabe. Genève: The Author, 1979.
Arabic Elementary Course, Volume One/Cours élémentaire de
  langue arabe, volume 1. Genève: The Author/Poésie Vivante,
  1982.
Arabic Elementary Course, Volume II (Annexes)/Cours élémen-
  taire de langue arabe, volume II (annexes). Genève: The Au-
  thor/Poésie Vivante, 1983.
Handwriting Exercise Book/Cahier d'écriture. Genève: The Author, 1984.
Dialogues Textbook I: Words of Everyday Use/Manuel de dia-
  logues I: vocabulaire courant. Genève: Institut d'enseignement
  de la langue arabe/Poésie Vivante, 1984.
Dialogues Textbook II: United Nations, Questions and Answers/
  Manuel de dialogues II: Les Nations Unies, questions et ré-
  ponses. Genève: Institut d'enseignement de la langue arabe/
  Poésie Vivante, 1984.
Dialogues Textbook III: Words of Everyday Use/Manuel de
  dialogues III: vocabulaire courant. Genève: The Author/Poésie
  Vivante, 1985. (Suite au Manuel I)

Nacereddine's Multilingual Dictionary: 2500 Arabic words of current usage with translation in 7 languages - English, Français, Español, Deutsch, Russkij, Chinese, Japanese. Geneva: The Author, 1991.

Alphabet illustré. Genève: The Author, 1996.

Arabic Pictorial/L'Illustré arabe. Geneva: The Author, 1996.

Chinese Pictorial/L'Illustré chinois. Geneva: The Author, 1997.

Russian Pictorial/L'Illustré russe. Geneva: The Author, 1997.

Interactive Arabic/Arabe interactif. Geneva: The Author, 2004. CD-ROM

Fundamental Arabic Textbook/Manuel d'Arabe fondamental. Rev. ed. Bloomington, IN: AuthorHouse, 2008.

Nouvelle approche de l'enseignement de la grammaire arabe. Bloomington, IN: AuthorHouse, 2009.

Manuel d'écriture et de prononciation arabes. Bloomington, IN: AuthorHouse, 2011.

Publications used in the United Nations, Geneva, Arabic Language Courses - not UN official publications

Grammatical Applications: Idioms and Locutions of Everyday Use/Applications grammaticales: idiomes et locutions d'usage courant. Geneva: 1980.

Arabic Language Course: Practical Exercises/Cours de langue arabe: exercices pratiques. Geneva: 1981.

Livre de conversation, première partie. Genève: 1981.

A Dictionary of International Relations (news-economics-politics)/Dictionnaire des relations internationales (actualités-économie-politique). Geneva: 1986.

A Basic Dictionary: Everyday Vocabulary/Dictionnaire de base: vocabulaire courant. Geneva: 1987. 2 v.

A New Approach to Arabic Grammar. Geneva: 1988.

Nouvelle approche de la grammaire arabe. Genève: 1988.

Handwriting and Pronunciation Handbook/Manuel d'écriture et de prononciation. Genève: 19911.

For further information, please visit
www.a-nacereddine.com

Abdallah Nacereddine

Handbook
of Arabic
Writing and
Pronunciation

عبد الله ناصر الدين

authorHOUSE®

AuthorHouse™
1663 Liberty Drive
Bloomington, IN 47403
www.authorhouse.com
Phone: 1-800-839-8640

First published by AuthorHouse 7/8/2011

ISBN: 978-1-4634-1482-5 (sc)
ISBN: 978-1-4634-1480-1 (e)

Library of Congress Control Number: 2011910045

Printed in the United States of America

INTRODUCTION

This ***Handbook of handwriting and pronunciation*** is the fruit of several years' teaching the Arabic language at the United Nations Office in Geneva and interaction with students from fifty different countries of the five continents, that is to say from different religions, cultures, and linguistic origins. It is the collection of lessons prepared one by one in order to reply specifically to the immediate needs of each student, taking into consideration his or her language of origin, job, intellectual level, training, etc.

The Arabic alphabet contains several letters and sounds which do not exist in other languages. Learners differentiate between them with difficulty and often confuse them.

Among these students are a certain number whose mother tongue is Persian, Urdu, or Pashto. They are keen to learn Arabic which is the language of the Koran. However, many are not interested in learning the Arabic alphabet, as they wrongly think that they know it sufficiently well, since it is the same alphabet that they use in their respective languages of origin, which they have learnt from an early age. Therefore, they do not think it is useful to learn it again like little children. This is their argument. They do not realise that, even if they can master Arabic, what they write must look like Arabic, and what they say, when they speak, must sound like Arabic, and not like Persian or Urdu. This is the reason why, whatever the language of origin of the

i

learner, I insist on good handwriting and good pronunciation from the very beginning, no matter how long it takes. Bad handwriting and faulty pronunciation cannot be corrected, if they are allowed to take hold.

It is true that these three languages, as well as others such as Kurdish, Sindhi, Sundanese, Uzbek, Uigur, and Turkish (until 1928), use the Arabic alphabet. But their writing and, even more so, their pronunciation are clearly different from Arabic.

This is why students whose mother tongue is Farsi (Persian), Urdu and Pashto are well advised to learn to write and to pronounce each letter of the Arabic alphabet like true beginners, rather than like false ones, if they seriously wish to study Arabic.

It is the same case with the Latin alphabet, although less accentuated. Let us take as an example the letter *J*, which is written in the same way, but is pronounced differently in English, French, German, and Spanish. In languages which use the Arabic alphabet, there are several letters which are written and pronounced differently.

In these languages, there are also words of Arabic origin, but they have different meanings. This is why it is advisable for students from countries where the language uses the Arabic alphabet to look up in the dictionary each Arabic word used in their language, in order to make sure of the meaning. Let us take as examples:

(a) The word *milla(t)* which means *community/confession/ religious doctrine, belief, religion* in Arabic. In Persian, the same word simply means *nation*;

(b) The word *mousafir* which means *traveller* in Arabic. In Turkish, pronounced *missafir*, it means *guest*;

(c) The word *lahm* which means *meat* in Arabic. In Hebrew, with a slightly different pronunciation, it means *bread*. Thus, in Arabic, the town of Bethlehem means *the house of meat*, while in Hebrew it means *the house of bread*. (However, it does not mean *butcher's shop* in Arabic, nor *baker's shop* in Hebrew. Another word is used in the two languages.)

This advice is valid for all students of the Arabic language whose language of origin does not use the Arabic alphabet, but which is of the same Semitic family, like Hebrew, or other languages which have no connection to Arabic, but which are influenced by Islam, such as Hindi, Malay, Swahili, Wolof (in Senegal), and the Berber languages, or by Arab-Islamic civilization, such as Maltese, Spanish, and Portuguese.

Often, the same words are found by pure chance in different languages, but with different meanings. Here are a few examples:

- The word *gift* in German means poison; in English, it means *present*.

iii

- The word *easy* in English means *fly* (insect) in Berber.
- The world *sakana* in Arabic means *to inhabit, to reside*; in Japanese, it means *fish*.

The following is a brief indication mainly of Persian and Urdu.

Persian

The sound of consonants and vowels in Persian is different from that of Arabic because Persian has no linguistic connection to Arabic. "It is one of the Iranian languages which form a branch of the Indo-European family. [...] The language was written in Cuneiform [...] In the 2nd century B.C. the Persians created their own alphabet, known as Pahlavi, which remained in use until the Islamic conquest of the 7th century. Since that time Persian has been written in the Arabic alphabet with a number of additional characters to accommodate special sounds."[1]

The same can be observed with the Greek alphabet which is used in Coptic as well as in Russian by adding a certain number of characters for special sounds.

However, Persian has kept the Arabic characters which do not exist in Persian. Persian vowels, though few, are easily recognisable to the ear, unlike Arabic vowels. The consonants are very different from Arabic ones. This is important, as certain Arabic letters are not recognized in Persian pronunciation.[2]

The Persian style of writing is different from Arabic handwriting, but it is very aesthetic. For this reason, it is often used for headings in Arabic, especially in newspapers. It is appreciated for its charm.

Kurdish and Pashto

The same rule applies to Kurdish and Pashto which are close to Persian, since they are part of the same family of Iranian languages.

Urdu

Urdu takes its name from the Turkish word *ordu* which means *army* and has given the word *horde* in English. Urdu is a Hindustani dialect, close to Hindi, which was the language spoken at the court of the Moghuls in the 17th century. Its name dates from this period, as it was the language of the imperial camp. Urdu is the official language of Pakistan but it is also a constitutional language of India. [3]

Urdu belongs to the native Indian tradition rather than to Arab-Persian culture. [4]

"A large number of Persian, Arabic, and Turkish words entered the language via the military camps and the marketplaces of Delhi." [5]

The cultural and linguistic environment in which I carried out my work was very useful to me, as it encouraged me to undertake further research into languages which I had started to study a long time previously. There are around twenty in all. I acquired more than 250 teaching methods consisting, in the beginning, of dictionaries, grammar textbooks, card files, audio cassettes, or records, and CD-ROMs, etc., later on.

Some students who had followed Arabic courses before with other teachers were surprised by my calmness when they made mistakes or had difficulties with pronunciation, handwriting, or memorisation. Their former teachers always became annoyed, going as far as to call them stupid sometimes, according to one student. For my part, I keep my cool for a simple and obvious reason. I could well understand them, since I myself was always learning a language with a new alphabet or a completely different system of writing. I experienced the same difficulties in writing, pronunciation, and memorisation. I met with the same problems and difficulties as them, so I was in the same dilemma. I do not become irritable or chide students when they make mistakes; on the contrary, I encourage them and congratulate them for all their efforts to learn. The teacher-student relationship should be the same as the relationship between a mother and a young child. If a mother becomes cross and scolds her child each time he stumbles or pronounces a word wrongly, he will not be able to walk or talk correctly. He will limp and stutter all his life.

I notice that most students are content with what they learn during lessons. Except for a few, they do not try to study by themselves. That is why I urge them to learn to study also on their own and not to depend wholly on the teacher. As I, myself, am self-taught, having learnt almost everything on my own, I simply ask them to follow my example.

I have applied myself to studying these languages naturally, not all at the same time, but one by one, devoting a certain time, some months or some years, to each language until I reached a total of twenty languages. Among these languages are my mother tongue, Berber, and principally Arabic, which I started to learn, almost like a foreign language, more or less only at the age of seventeen, even though I learned the Koran by heart – without understanding a single word, however. There are several other languages which I have not studied but about which I have learned a great deal, thanks to my students.

Often my students asked me desperately:
- Are we really going to learn this language one day?
With great enthusiasm, I would reply:
- Yes, you will learn it; that is for sure.
- How can you confirm that?
- Since I have learned it, you will also succeed (explaining at the same time my argument).

I may have surprised them, but I am not sure that I convinced them.

When I undertook to study all these languages, my aim,

for some of them, was to master them in order to speak, write, and read them. For others, it was only to know their writing system, their structure, their morphology, the basics of grammar, their historical origins, etc. In this way, when I talk to certain people of my two multilingual dictionaries, each containing eight modern languages – the first published in 1991, the second unpublished – they ask me, "Do speak all these languages?" My answer is, "No."

In the same way, when I pointed out that my dictionary contains everyday words, they also asked me, "Give us an example." I replied that that depended for whom. For example, the word *snow*, which has twelve different colours, is an everyday word for Eskimos. For a Targui (pl. Touareg), the word *camel* is an everyday word and has a thousand names. For a Korean, there are four different words for the everyday word *rice*. [6]

Even more interesting is the symbolism in Chinese which does not use an alphabet but ideograms, which have been adopted by the Japanese language, but with a different pronunciation. Originally, they were images before undergoing several modifications in order to simplify them. For example, (a) the ideogram for *friend, friendship* "represents the right hands of two friends, acting in the same direction [7]; (b) the ideogram for *good order, peace* represents women enclosed in a house." [8]

To know a language is to know the mentality, the way of

viii

thinking and of expressing himself, the customs, and the life style of the person who speaks that language. It is never possible to know and understand a people without knowing its language, even basically, even if you live with that people all your life. However, if you learn its language, you can know and understand the people, and so love it, without necessarily living among it. By studying its language and its culture, you can identify with it and become an integral part of its heritage. All the prejudices, the preconceived ideas, the reproaches, and the criticisms vanish. Often the French think that Arabs are rude when they use the familiar form of address (*tu*) or when they use the first person first, saying *I and you* instead of *you and I.* When they learn Arabic, they understand that the person is only beginning to study French and is not yet familiar with their culture, that the polite form of address used in French does not exist in Arabic, and that it is usual to start with the first person.*

In the same way, a beginner of Korean or Japanese, for example, may shock the people he is speaking to, if he does not

---

*The personal pronoun for the second person plural (*you*) exists in Arabic. There are even three types of plural *you:* (a) you two men or you two women, or you two, a man and a woman; (b) you three or more men; (c) you three or more women. That is why it is advisable for a French speaker, if he wishes to invite an Arab friend or colleague, to use the appropriate personal pronoun (singular or plural) or say clearly *you and your wife*, if he wishes to invite a couple. If he says *I invite you*, using the polite form of address, he takes the risk of finding the whole family on his doorstep!

take into account who is speaking to whom. In many languages of the world, especially in the Far East, the same sentence can be very different according to the social relations of the speakers. [9]

It is possible to know in depth any people by learning its language, not only existing peoples, but also people who lived thousands of years ago but who have totally disappeared, such as the ancient Egyptians.

Egyptologists have studied hieroglyphics. Through this language which they have studied in detail, they have learned all about the customs and life style of the Egyptians in Antiquity. They probably know more about them than about their contemporaries, the Egyptians today, with whom they are constantly in contact when they carry out their research in Egypt, if they have no knowledge of Arabic or Coptic. Knowledge of Coptic may also help in understanding better the Coptic Christians who now speak Arabic only but who use Coptic, which descends from Ancient Egyptian, as the language of their Church. [10]

But how can someone realize that he knows in depth the language and culture of a people? He can carry out the following test: When a native English-speaker, for example, who knows French, sees the word *arbre* written, he thinks of a *tree*; he imagines it vividly before him, rather than merely as a word which means *tree* in English.

Thanks to my familiarity with, and my knowledge – even basic – of so many languages, I was able to understand the difficulties encountered by each one of my students, so I used every means to remedy them.

To sum up: If you tell me what your mother tongue is, I can anticipate the mistakes you will make in Arabic. In the same way, from the mistakes you make in Arabic, I can tell you your mother tongue.

My students have obviously taught me many things, perhaps without knowing it. This is not only my case. Every teacher learns from his students. This means that one is never 100% teacher, nor 100% student, but both at the same time, not only in the classroom, but also in everyday life. We are all teaching each other without cease, without being conscious of this.

This Handbook is not a treatise on comparative linguistics. However, instead of dealing only with the languages which use the Arabic alphabet, I refer to other languages, since I find that there are common features which every student of Arabic must know, whatever his language of origin, whether or not it uses the Arabic alphabet.

Geneva, March 1st, 2011   Abdallah Nacereddine

Bibliographical references

1. Katzner, Kenneth. *The Languages of the World*. London: Routledge, 1986, p. 166-7.

2. Malherbe, Michel. *Les langages de l'humanité*. Paris: Seghers, 1983, p. 178.

3. Ibid., p. 187.

4. Campbell, George L. *Concise Compendium of the World's Languages*. London: Routledge, 1998, p. 562.

5. Katzner, Kenneth. *Op. cit.*, p. 179.

6. Malherbe, Michel ; Tellier, Oliver ; Choi Jung Wha. *Parlons coréen*. Paris : Editions L'Harmattan, p. 228.

7. Wieger, L. *Chinese Characters : Their Origin, Etymology, History, Classification and Signification*. New York: Dover Publications, 1965, p. 122.

8. Ibid, p. 169.

9. Malherbe, Michel ; Tellier, Oliver ; Choi Jung Wha. *Op. cit.*, p. 45.

10. Malherbe, Michel. *Op. cit.*, p. 417.

Contents

المحتويات

The Alphabet

الحروف الهجائية

ا	ب	ت	ث
ج	ح	خ	د
ذ	ر	ز	س
ش	ص	ض	ط
ظ	ع	غ	ف
ق	ك	ل	م
ن	ه	و	ي
لا	ء		

ب Bāʼ B book	ا Alif A, U/O, I at, on, it
ث Ṯāʼ TH think	ت Tāʼ T time
ح Ḥāʼ no equivalent	ج Ǧīm J (Dj) June
د Dāl D deed	خ Ḫāʼ Spanish Jota ojo

4

ر

Rā'
R
room

ذ

Ḏāl
TH
that

س

Sīn
S
seat

ز

Zai
Z
zone

ص

Ṣād
S (emphatic)
salt

ش

Šīn
SH
sheet

ط

Ṭā'
T (emphatic)
talk

ض

Ḍād
D (emphatic)
doll

5

ع	ظ
^cain no equivalent	Ẓa' TH (emphatic) those

ف	غ
Fā' F fat	Ḡin Fr. r (grasséyé) rire

ك	ق
Kāf K cat	Qāf no equivalent

م	ل
Mīm M man	Lām L life

6

هـ

Hā'
H
hat

ن

Nūn
N
noon

ي

Yā'
Y
yes

و

Wāw
W
woman

ء

Hamza
A, U/O, I
at, on, it

لا

Lāmalif
Combination of two
letters : ل et ا

Part One
Writing

القسم الأول
الخط/الكتابة

Separate	Final	Medial	Initial

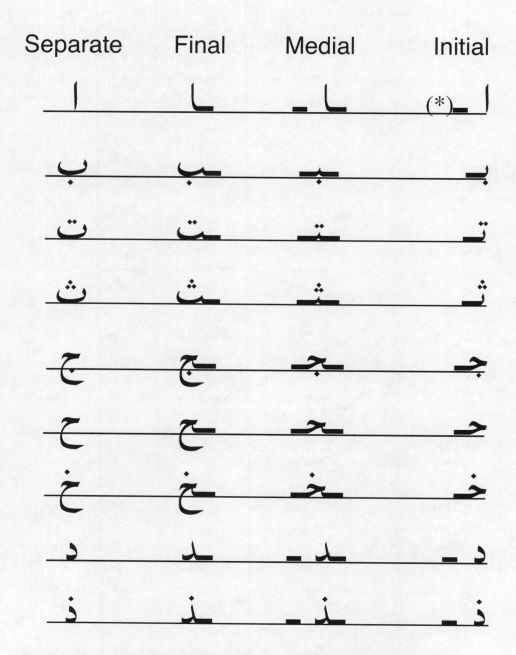

(*) The line marks the position of the following letter meaning that the precedent letter does not attach to it.

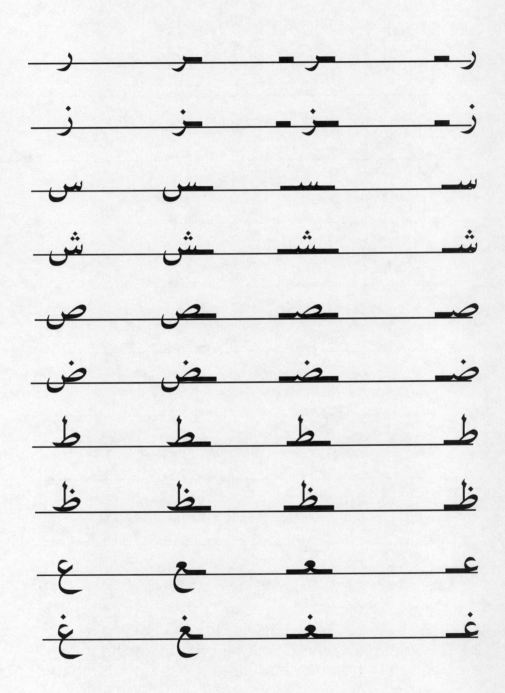

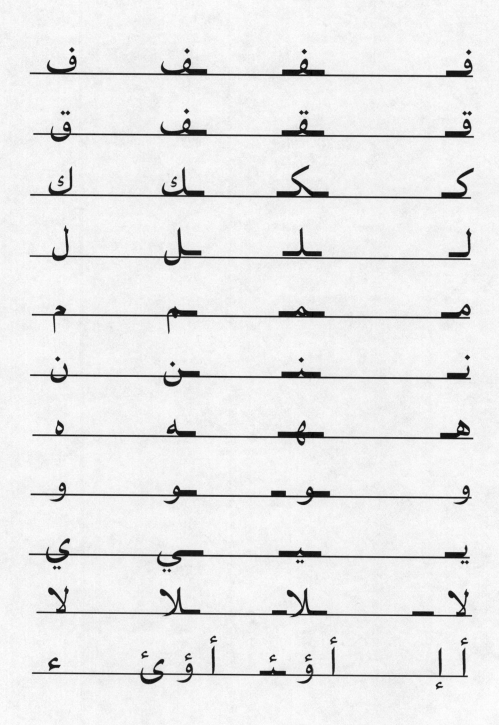

13

Writing
Exercises

تمارين في
الخط/الكتابة

Separate	Final	Medial	Initial	
قَرَأَ	نَبَأٌ	سَأَلَ	أَكَلَ	ا :
شَرِبَ	كَتَبَ	جَبَلٌ	بِنْتٌ	ب :
بَاتَ	بِنْتٌ	فَتَحَ	تَمْرٌ	ت :
حَرَثَ	مَكَثَ	مَثَلٌ	ثَلْجٌ	ث :
خَرَجَ	نَسَجَ	نَجَحَ	جَبَلٌ	ج :
صَاحَ	فَتَحَ	بَحَثَ	حَبْلٌ	ح :
دَاخَ	فَخْرٌ	خَرَجَ	خَبَرٌ	خ :
بَرْدٌ	وَلَدٌ	قَدَمٌ	دَخَلَ	د :
عَاذَ	نَفَذَ	بَذَلَ	ذَهَبَ	ذ :
سَارَ	خَبَرٌ	شَرِبَ	رَجُلٌ	ر :

17

Separate	Final	Medial	Initial	
فَرَز	قَفَزَ	نَزَلَ	زَلَقَ	ز :
غَرَسَ	جَلَس	غَسَلَ	سَكَنَ	س :
فَرْش	عطش	نَشَرَ	شَرَبَ	ش :
قُرْصٌ	فَحَصَ	فَصْلٌ	صَبَرَ	ص :
فَاض	رَفَضَ	حَضَرَ	ضَرَبَ	ض :
شَرْطٌ	سَقَطَ	نَطَقَ	طَلَبَ	ط :
غَاظ	حَفِظَ	نَظَرَ	ظَهَرَ	ظ :
بَاعَ	سَمِعَ	لَعِبَ	عَرَفَ	ع :
فَرَغَ	بَلَغَ	شَغَلَ	غَسَلَ	غ :
عَرَف	كَشَف	كَفَلَ	فَهِمَ	ف :

Separate	Final	Medial	Initial	
بَرْقٌ	سَبَقَ	نَقَلَ	قَدَمٌ : ق
تَرَكَ	سَمَكٌ	سَكَنَ	كَتَبَ : ك
نَزَلَ	رَجُلٌ	جَلَسَ	لَعِبَ : ل
قَدَمٌ	فَهِمَ	عَمِلَ	مَثَلٌ : م
قَرْنٌ	سَكَنَ	بِنْتٌ	نَزَلَ : ن
بَدَهَ	وَجْهٌ	فَهِمَ	هَرَبَ : هـ
فَرْوٌ	بَهْوٌ	يَوْمٌ	وَجَدَ : و
شَايٌ	كُرْسِي	عَيْن	يَوْمٌ : ي
إِلَّا	عَلَّا	سَلَامٌ	لَازِم : لا
مَاءٌ	بِئْرٌ	سُؤَالٌ	أَبٌ إِمَامٌ : ء
فَتَاةٌ	سَنَةٌ		: ة

19

Note on writing

مَلْحُوظَةٌ بِخُصُوصِ الْكِتَابَةِ

All the letters of the Arabic alphabet, whether handwritten or printed, are linked together. However seven are only linked to the preceding letters, not to the following ones. These letters are the following:

ا د ذ ر ز و لا .

For this reason, there are two types of finals: linked and separate, depending on the preceding linked or detached letter, as shown by the following example:

. عمل، نزل

Semi-attached letters

الحروف شبه المنفصلة

Separate	Final	Medial	Initial
ا	ـا	ـاـ	ا ـ
بَدَا	نَمَا	سَالَ	إِسْمٌ
د	ـد	ـدـ	د ـ
عَادَ	وَلَدٌ	قَدَمٌ	دَخَلَ
ذ	ـذ	ـذـ	ذ ـ
عَاذَ	نَفَذَ	بَذَلَ	ذَهَب
ر	ـر	ـرـ	ر ـ
صَارَ	خَبَرٌ	شَرِب	رَجُلٌ
ز	ـز	ـزـ	ز ـ
مَوْزٌ	قَفَزَ	نَزَلَ	زَرَعَ

22

Separate	Final	Medial	Initial
و	ـو	ـوـ	و ـ
فَرْوٌ	بَهْوٌ	يَوْمٌ	وَلَدٌ
لا	ـلا	ـلاـ	لا ـ
إِلَّا	عَلَا	سَلَامٌ	لَازِمٌ

Remark: These letters are attached to the preceding but not to the following.

Note concerning
the distinction between
certain letters

مَلْحُوظَةٌ بِخُصُوصِ التَّمْيِيزِ
بَيْنَ بَعْضِ الْحُرُوفِ

Note that certain letters (in pairs or in triads) are identical. They are distinguished only by the number of the dots: one, two or three, and the position: under the letter or above the letter.

Others are slightly different. They are written in final or separate, either on the line or under the line.

See the following table:

Semi-homogeneous letters (1)

الحروف المتجانسة (١)

ب

ت

ث

ن

ي

Separate	Final	Medial	Initial
ب	ـب	ـبـ	بـ
شَرِب	كَتَبَ	جَبَلٌ	بِنْت
ت	ـت	ـتـ	تـ
صَوْتٌ	بِنْتُ	فَتَح	تَبِعَ
ث	ـث	ثـ	ثـ
حَدَثَ	بَحَثَ	مَثَلٌ	ثَلْجٌ
ن	ـن	ـنـ	نـ
قَرْنٌ	سَكَنَ	بِنْتُ	نَزَلَ
ي	ـي	ـيـ	يـ
شَايُّ	نَقِي	عَيْن	يَوْمٌ

27

Semi-homogeneous letters (1)

الحروف شبه المتجانسة (١)

ع

غ

ف

ق

و

Separate	Final	Medial	Initial
ع	ع	ـعـ	عـ
بَاعَ	سَمِعَ	لَعِب	عَمِلَ
غ	ـغ	ـغـ	غـ
فَرَغَ	بَلَغَ	شَغَل	غَسَلَ
ف	ـف	ـفـ	فـ
عَرَف	كَشَفَ	كَفَلَ	فَهِمَ
ق	ـق	ـقـ	قـ
شَرْقٌ	سَبَقَ	نَقَلَ	قَلْبٌ
و	ـو	ـو	و
فَرْوٌ	بَهْوٌ	يَوْمٌ	وَلَدٌ

31

Homogeneous
letters (2)
(pairs and triads)

الحروف المتجانسة (٢)

(أزواجا وثواليث)

١) ب ت ث

٢) ج ح خ

٣) د ذ

٤) ر ز

٥) س ش

٦) ص ض

٧) ط ظ

٨) ع غ

٩) ة ه

١) ب	شَرِبَ	كَتَبَ	جَبَلٌ	بِنْتٌ	ب
	صَوْتٌ	بِنْتُ	فَتَحَ	تَمْرٌ	ت
	حَرَثَ	مَكَثَ	مَثَلٌ	ثَلْجٌ	ث
٢) ج	خَرَجَ	نَسَجَ	نَجَحَ	جَبَلٌ	ج
	رُوحٌ	فَتَحَ	بَحَثَ	حَبْلٌ	ح
	دَاخَ	نَسَخَ	خَرَجَ	خَبَرٌ	خ
٣) د	بَرْدٌ	وَلَدٌ	قَدَمٌ	دَخَلَ	د
	عَاذَ	نَفَذَ	بَذَلَ	ذَهَبَ	ذ
٤) ر	سَارَ	خَبَرَ	شَرِبَ	رَجُلٌ	ر
	فَرَزَ	قَفَزَ	نَزَلَ	زَلِقَ	ز

35

٥) س   سَكَنَ غَسَلَ جَلَسَ غَرَسَ

ش   شَرِبَ نَشَرَ عَطِشَ فَرَشَ

٦) ص   صَبَرَ فَصْلٌ فَحَصَ قُرْصٌ

ض   ضَرَبَ حَضَرَ رَفَضَ مَرَضَ

٧) ط   طَلَبَ نَطَقَ سَقَطَ شَرْطٌ

ظ   ظَهَرَ نَظَرَ حَفِظَ غَاظَ

٨) ع   عَمِلَ لَعِبَ سَمِعَ بَاعَ

غ   غَسَلَ شَغَلَ بَلَغَ فَرِغَ

٩) ة   مَدِينَةٌ فَتَاةٌ

ه   وَجْهٌ بَدَهَ

36

Semi-homogeneous letters (2)
(divided into groups)

الحروف المتجانسة (٢)

(مقسمة إلى مجموعات)

١) ا ل

٢) ب ت ث ن ي

٣) ث ش

٤) د ذ ر ز

٥) ص ض ط ظ

٦) ع غ ف ق م و

١) ١   قَرَأَ   نَبَأَ   سَأَلَ   أَكَلَ   ا

ل   نَزَلَ   رَجُلٌ   جَلَسَ   لَعِبَ   ل

٢) ب   شَرِبَ   كَتَبَ   جَبَلٌ   بِنْتٌ   ب

ت   صَوْتٌ   بِنْتٌ   فَتَحَ   تَمْرٌ   ت

ث   حَرَثَ   مَكَثَ   مَثَلٌ   ثَلْجٌ   ث

ن   قَرْنٌ   سَكَنَ   بِنْتٌ   نَزَلَ   ن

ي   شَايٌّ   كُرْسِيٌّ   عَيْنٌ   يَوْمٌ   ي

٣) ث   عَاثَ   مَكَثَ   نَثْرٌ   ثُلُثٌ   ث

ش   عَاشَ   عَطِشَ   نَشَرَ   شَرِبَ   ش

39

٤) د   دَخَلَ   قَدَمٌ   وَلَدٌ   بَرْدٌ

ذ   ذَهَبَ   بَذَلَ   نَفَذَ   عَاذَ

ر   رَجُلٌ   شَرِبَ   خَبَرٌ   سَارَ

ز   زَلَقَ   نَزَلَ   قَفَزَ   فَرَزَ

٥) ص   صَبَرَ   فَصْلٌ   فَحَصَ   قُرْصٌ

ض   ضَرَبَ   حَضَرَ   رَفَضَ   مَرَضٌ

ط   طَلَبَ   نَطَقَ   سَقَطَ   شَرْطٌ

ظ   ظَهَرَ   نَظَرَ   حَفِظَ   غَاظَ

٦)	ع	عَمِلَ	لَعِبَ	سَمِعَ	بَاعَ
	غ	غَسَلَ	شَغَلَ	بَلَغَ	فَرَغَ
	ف	فَهِمَ	شَغَلَ	كَشَفَ	عَرَفَ
	ق	قَدَّمَ	نَقَلَ	سَبَقَ	بَرْقٌ
	م	مَثَلٌ	عَمِلَ	فَهِمَ	قَدَّمَ
	و	وَجْهٌ	يَوْمٌ	بَهْوٌ	فَرْوٌ

Part Two
Pronunciation

القسم الثاني

النطق

THE ALPHABET الحروف الهجائية
THE SOUND الصوت

Symbol	Name of the letter	Transli-teration		Symbol	Name of the letter	Transli-teration
ض	Ḍad	ḍ		ء	Hamza (1)	'a, u, ı
ط	Ṭa'	ṭ		ا	'Alif (2)	'a, u, ı
ظ	Ẓa'	ẓ		ب	Ba'	b
ع	ɛain	ʕ		ت	Ta'	t
غ	Gain	ḡ		ث	Ṯa'	ṯ
ف	Fa'	f		ج	Ǧim	ǧ
ق	Qaf	q		ح	Ḥa'	ḥ
ك	Kaf	k		خ	Ḫa'	ḫ
ل	Lam	l		د	Dal	d
م	Mim	m		ذ	Ḏal	ḏ
ن	Nun	n		ر	Ra'	r
ه	Ha'	h		ز	Zay	z
و	Waw	w		س	Sin	s
ي	Ya'	y		ش	Šin	š
لا	lamalif	la		ص	Ṣad	ṣ

(1) Glottal stop. (2) Otherwise, *'alif* is used as a lomg vowel.

45

The short vowels
اَلْحَرَكَاتُ

The Arabs had originally no signs for short vowels. At a later period, the following signs were invented to express them:

a) *fatḥa* ــَ is a sign written above the consonant having the value of a, as in *man.*

b) *kasra* ــِ is a sign written below the consonant having the value of i, as in *this.*

c) *ḍamma* ــُ is a sign written above the consonant having the value of u, as in *full.*

kasra   ḍamma   fatḥa

اَلْفَتْحَةُ ـَ اَلضَّمَّةُ ـُ اَلْكَسْرَةُ ـِ

خِ خُ خَ   أَ أُ إِ

دِ دُ دَ   بَ بُ بِ

ذِ ذُ ذَ   تَ تُ تِ

رِ رُ رَ   ثَ ثُ ثِ

زِ زُ زَ   جَ جُ جِ

سِ سُ سَ   حَ حُ حِ

47

قِ	قُ	قَ	شِ	شُ	شَ
كِ	كُ	كَ	صِ	صُ	صَ
لِ	لُ	لَ	ضِ	ضُ	ضَ
مِ	مُ	مَ	طِ	طُ	طَ
نِ	نُ	نَ	ظِ	ظُ	ظَ
هِ	هُ	هَ	عِ	عُ	عَ
وِ	وُ	وَ	غِ	غُ	غَ
يِ	يُ	يَ	فِ	فُ	فَ

The gutturals
حُرُوفُ الْحَلْقِ

The guttural letters are:

ء *hamza* (Chap. 11).

ح *ḥā'* is a strongly guttural letter *h* produced by a strong expulsion of air from the chest. It should not be confused with :

خ *ḫā'* which is a guttural *ch* as in the Scottish "*loch*" and the German "*Aachen*".

ع *ain* is a very strong guttural, produced by compression of the throat and expulsion of breath.

غ *ain* is the sound made in gargling or like the French "*r*" grasseyé with a little more of the "*g*".

ه *hā'* represents the same sound as does English *h*.

49

أَ أُ إِ
حَ حُ حِ
خَ خُ خِ
عَ عُ عِ
غَ غُ غِ
قَ قُ قِ
هَ هُ هِ

Remark : The grammarians give only five letters ح خ ع غ هـ as gutturals.

The emphatics
اَلْحُرُوفُ الْمُضَخَّمَةُ

ص *ṣād* ض *ḍād,* ط *ṭā'* and ظ *ẓā'* form a group of emphatic sounds corresponding to س *sīn* ت *tā'* and ذ *ḏāl.*

In pronouncing them, the tongue is pressed against the edge of the upper teeth, and then withdrawn forcefully.

It should be noted that, with these emphatic consonants, the sound of *fatḥa* tends to be that of *a* in father; the sound of *kasra* tends to be that of *e* in *tell*; the sound *ḍamma* tends to be that of *oa* in *boat.*

صِ صُ صَ

ضِ ضُ ضَ

طِ طُ طَ

ظِ ظُ ظَ

The difference
in pronunciation
between emphatic
letters and the
corresponding
non-emphatic letters

التمييز في النطق بين

بعض الحروف المضخمة

وغيرالمضخمة المتجانسة

تَ - طَ - ذَ - ظَ

تُ - طُ - ذُ - ظُ

تِ - طِ - ذِ - ظِ

دَ - ضَ - سَ - صَ

دُ - ضُ - سُ - صُ

دِ - ضِ - سِ - صِ

The difference
in pronunciation
between emphatic
and non-emphatic
letters, in relation
to the learner's
linguistic origin

التمييز في النطق بين

بعض الحروف حسب

لغة الدارس الأصلية

ثَ – ذَ

ثُ – ذُ

ث – ذ

ذَ – زَ – ظَ

ذُ – زُ – ظُ

ذِ – زِ – ظِ

رَ – غَ

رُ – غُ

رِ – غِ

لَ – رَ

لُ – رُ

ل – ر

سَ – زَ

سُ – زُ

سِ – زِ

كَ – قَ

كُ – قُ

كِ – قِ

The long vowels
حُرُوفُ الْمَدِّ

The long vowels or the lengthening letters are the following:

ا 'alif for the lengthening of the consonant having as a short vowel ـَ fatḥa, e. g. دَا dā.

و waw for the lengthening of the consonant having as a short vowel ـُ ḍamma, e.g. دُو dū.

ي yā' for the lengthening of the consonant having as a short vowel ـِ kasra e.g. دِي dī.

ـِي	تُوْ	ـَا
تِينٌ	تُوتٌ	بَابٌ
نِيرٌ	نُورٌ	نَارٌ
فِيلٌ	فُولٌ	جَارٌ
جِيلٌ	سُوقٌ	حَالٌ
طِينٌ	طُولٌ	خَالٌ
دِينٌ	دُورٌ	عَامٌ
عِيدٌ	كُوبٌ	بَالٌ
رِيحٌ	رُوحٌ	دَارٌ
كِيسٌ	قُوتٌ	شَايٌ

The distinction
between
the short vowels
and the long vowels

التمييز بين

الحركات القصيرة

والحركات الطويلة

وَاصَلَ	وَصَلَ
نَاصَبَ	نَصَبَ
أُذُونٌ	أُذُنٌ
رُبُوعٌ	رُبُعٌ
سَافَرَ	سَفَرَ
عَادَلَ	عَدَلَ
عَاكَسَ	عَكَسَ
رَافَعَ	رَفَعَ
ذَهَابٌ	ذَهَبٌ
عَالَمٌ	عَلَمٌ

Letters used
sometimes as
lengthening letters
and sometimes
as consonants

ا - و - ي

الحروف التي تستخدم

كحركات طويلة أحيانا

وكصوامت أحيانا أخر

ا - و - ي

ثَارَ – ثَأَرَ	عُودٌ – أَعْوَادٌ	
سَالَ – سَأَلَ	سِيرَةَ – سِيَرٌ	
زَارَ – زَأَرَ	قِيمَةٌ – قِيَمٌ	
بَدَا – بَدَأَ	مِيلٌ – أَمْيَالٌ	
نَبَا – نَبَأَ	فِيلٌ – فُيُولٌ	
فُوطَةٌ – فُوطٌ	جِيلٌ – أَجْيَالٌ	
سُوقٌ – أَسْوَاقٌ	مِرْآةٌ	
دُورٌ – أَدْوَارٌ	طَاوُوسٌ	
عِيدٌ – أَعْيَادٌ	تَمْيِيزٌ	

62

Tašdīd or *Šadda*
or Stressing

اَلشَّدَّةُ

A consonant that is to be doubled is written once, but marked with the sign ّ which is called *šadda* or *tašdīd,* e.g. مَدَّ *madda, to extend.*

بَلَّغَ	حَدَّ	شَدَّ
قَسَّمَ	وَدَّ	عَدَّ
كَبَّرَ	شَدَّدَ	مَلَّ
تَكَلَّمَ	قَرَّرَ	قَلَّ
تَقَبَّلَ	سَكَّنَ	رَدَّ
حَدَّدَ	فَضَّلَ	ظَنَّ
مَوَادُّ	سَجَّلَ	شَمَّ
صَدَّرَ	عَلَّمَ	شَكَّ
وَدَّعَ	قَدَّمَ	صَبَّ

Tanwīn
اَلتَّنْوِينُ

The marks of the short vowels when doubled are pronounced with the addition of the sound *n*.

ـٌ *un,* ـٍ *in,* ـً *an*.

This is called *tanwīn* or *nunation* (from the name of the letter ن (*nūn*), and it takes its place only at the end of nouns and adjectives.

Note that *fatḥa* with the letter *ʿalif* is added to support the *tanwīn* ـً after all the consonants except ة *tāʾ marbuṭa*, ء and ى *ʿalif maqṣūra* (i.e. without diacritic points).

دَرْسٌ

قَلَمٌ

كِتَابٌ

مَرْحَباً

شُكْراً

عَفْواً

قَاضٍ

مُحَامٍ

كَافٍ

66

Sukūn
اَلسُّكُونُ

The *sukūn* ْـ is a small circle over the letter that indicates the absence of a vowel, e.g. كُنْ *kun, be.* It cannot follow the long vowels, except, rarely, in certain forms of the *doubled verb.*

كُنْ

قُلْ

كُلْ

اقْرَأْ

فَأْرُ

بِئْرٌ

نَعِمْ

مَنْ

كَيْفَ

68

Hamza
اَلْهَمْزَةُ

The *hamza* ء represents a glottal stop
produced by completely closing the vocal
chords and then by suddenly separating
them. The rules for the writing of *hamza* are
complicated. Explanations are given in another chapter, in another manual. Here, a
few guiding points will be mentioned.

Initial *hamza* is always written on or under *'alif* e.g. أَ '*a*, أُ '*u*, إِ '*i*.

In the middle or at the end of word,
hamza may be written separately or over
'alif, waw or *yā'* (without the two dots),
e.g. ء , أ , ؤ , ئ .

69

دائماً	فَأْرُ	أَبُّ
هَيَّأَ	بِئْرُ	أُمُّ
رَئِيسُ	بُؤْرَةُ	إِسْمُ
رِئَاسَةٌ	سُؤَالُ	سَأَلَ
مُخْطِئُ	تَفَاؤُلُ	نَبَأُ
هُدُوءُ	إِمْرَأَةُ	مَسْأَلَةٌ
بَطِيءُ	بِيئَةٌ	بَدَأَ
جُزْءُ	فِئَةُ	قَرَأَ
شَيْءُ	لُجُوءُ	مَأْوَى

Madda

اَلْمَدَّةُ

    If a *hamza* with *fatha* is followed by the long vowel *'alif*, the *hamza* and *fatha* are dropped, and the long vowel *'alif* is written over the *'alif* horizontally, thus: آ *'ā* instead of اأ. This is called *madda.*

    This also occurs when, at the begin-ning of a syllable, an *'alif* with *hamza* and *fatha* is followed by an *'alif* with *sukūn*, thus: آ *'ā* for اأ.

آمَالٌ	آبُ
مِرْآةٌ	آمَنَ
اَلْقُرْآنُ	آخَرُ
آسَى	آجُرُ
آذَارُ	اَلْآنَ
آدَمُ	آلَةُ
آثَارُ	آنِسَةٌ
اَلْآرَامِيّونَ	آبَارُ
مِرْآةٌ	آسِفٌ

72

The lunar letters
اَلْحُرُوفُ الْقَمَرِيَّةُ

The initial lunar letters of a noun do not assimilate the article that precedes them and do not receive *tašdīd*. They are also 14 in number:

أ ب ج ح خ ع غ ف ق ك م هـ و ي

Thus, one writes اَلْقَمَرُ *al-qamaru, the moon,* and one reads اَلْقَمَرُ *al-qamaru,* exactly the same way as one writes. Therefore, the initial consonant ق does not receive *tašdīd* and the consonant ل of the article maintains its *sukūn*.

These fourteen letters are called *lunar letters,* because the word قَمَرُ *moon,* happens to begin with one of them.

اَلْأَبُ	أَبٌ
اَلْبِنْتُ	بِنْتٌ
اَلْجَبَلُ	جَبَلٌ
اَلْحَلِيبُ	حَلِيبٌ
اَلْخَرِيفُ	خَرِيفٌ
اَلْعَيْنُ	عَيْنٌ
اَلْغَرْبُ	غَرْبٌ

اَلْفَمُ	فَمٌ
اَلْقَمَرُ	قَمَرٌ
اَلْكِتَابُ	كِتَابٌ
اَلْمَاءُ	مَاءٌ
اَلْهَوَاءُ	هَوَاءٌ
اَلْوَلَدُ	وَلَدٌ
اَلْيَدُ	يَدٌ

The solar letters
اَلْحُرُوفُ الشَّمْسِيَّةِ

The initial solar letters of nouns assimilate the article that precedes them and receive the euphonic *tašdīd*. They are 14 in number.

ت ث د ذ ر ز س ش ص ض ط ظ ل

Instead of الشَّمْسُ *al-šamsu the sun*, one writes اَلـشَّمْسُ with the *tašdīd* of the initial consonant ش and pronounces it *aš-šamsu*. The consonant ل, loses its *sukūn* and though expressed in writing, is not pronounced; it is assimilated to the next solar letter. These letters are called *the solar letters*, because the word شَمْسُ *sun* happens to begin with one of them.

اَلتَّمْرُ	تَمْرُ
اَلثَّوْبُ	ثَوْبُ
اَلدَّرْسُ	دَرْسُ
اَلذَّوْقُ	ذَوْقُ
اَلرَّجُلُ	رَجُلُ
اَلزَّمِيلُ	زَمِيلُ
اَلسَّلَامُ	سَلَامُ

77

اَلشَّمْسُ	شَمْسٌ
اَلصَّدِيقُ	صَدِيقٌ
اَلضَّيْفُ	ضَيْفٌ
اَلطَّالِبُ	طَالِبٌ
اَلظَّلَامُ	ظَلَامٌ
اَللَّيْلُ	لَيْلٌ
اَلنُّورُ	نُورٌ

78

Reading Exercises
Everyday words
Names of countries
and cities
Arabic terms of English
or French origin
English or French terms
of Arabic origin

تمارين في القراءة

أسماء مدن وبلدان

ألفاظ عربية من أصل فرنسي

ألفاظ فرنسية من أصل عربي

جِنِيفْ - بَارِيسُ - لَنْدَنُ - تُونِسُ

عُمَّانُ - مِصْرُ - كَنَدَا - إِفْرِيقِيَا

آسِيَا - أَمْرِيكَا - أُورُوبَا - سُورِيَا

رُوسِيَا - لُبْنَانُ - بَيْرُوتُ - رُومَا

مَدْرِيدُ - إِيطَالِيَا - أَبُوظَبِي - تُرْكِيَا

آذَرْبِيجَانُ - بَغْدَادُ - أَثِينَا - فَرَنْسَا

بَيْتَ لَحْمْ - عَمَّانُ - اَلْمَغْرِبُ - بُونْ

اَلْخُرْطُومُ - جَدَّةُ - اَلرِّيَاضُ - لَاهَايْ

صَنْعَاءُ - اَلسِّنِغَالُ - اَلسُّودَانُ - قَطَرُ

اَلْأُرْدُنُ - اَلْجَزَائِرُ - أَلْمَانِيَا - مَالِيزِيَا

اَلْقَاهِرَةُ - اَلْكُوَيْتُ - اَلْعِرَاقُ - طَهْرَانُ

لِيبِيَا - دِمَشْقُ - بَاكِسْتَانُ - اَلْهِنْدُ

كِيمِيَا - فِيزِيَا - جَبْرُ - كُحُولُ - سُكَّرُ

أَرُزُّ - قِيثَارُ - أَمِيرُ الْبَحْرِ - فُوسْفَات

تِكْنُولُوجِيَا - دُكْتُورُ - بِتْرُولُ - تِلِفُونْ

بِيرُوقْرَاطِيَا - تِلِفِزْيُونُ - مِتْرُ - كِيلُومِتْرُ

دِمُقْرَاطِيَةُ - رَادِيُو - غِرَامُ - كِيلُوغْرَامُ

بِيُولُوجِيَا - جُغْرَافِيَا - مَاكِينَةُ - بَنْكُ

أُورْكِسْتْرَا - سِمْفُونِيَةُ - بِيَانُو - دِيوَانُ

سِينَاتُورُ - فَيْلَسُوفُ - أَسْمَنْتُ - سِينَمَا

طَمَاطِمُ - قُنْصُلُ - بَرْلَمَانْ - مَخْزِنُ

قُبْطَانْ - كَارِيكَاتُورُ - لِتْرُ - بُرْتُقَالُ

81

Word-pairs
seemingly close
sound-wise for a
learner according
to his or her native
language

أزواج الكلمات
تبدو متقاربة صوتيا
لكل دارس حسب
لغته الأصلية

١٢) ذ - ز	١) أ - ع
١٣) ذ - ظ	٢) أ - هـ
١٤) ر - غ	٣) ت - ط
١٥) ر - ل	٤) ث - ذ
١٦) ز - س	٥) ث - س
١٧) س - ص	٦) ج - ش
١٨) ض - ط	٧) ح - خ
١٩) ع - غ	٨) ح - ع
٢٠) ع - هـ	٩) ح - هـ
٢١) غ - ق	١٠) خ - غ
٢٢) ق - ك	١١) د - ض

84

أ - هـ (٢)	أ - ع (١)
أَمَلَ - هَمَل	أَمَلٌ - عَمَلٌ
بَدَأَ - بَدَه	أَلَمٌ - عَلَمٌ
أَوَى - هَوَى	سَأَلَ - سَعَلَ
زَأَرَ - زَهَرَ	جَاءَ - جَاعَ
نَبَّأَ - نَبَّهَ	بَدَأَ - بَدَعَ
أَدَّبَ - هَدَّبَ	تَأَلَّمَ - تَعَلَّمَ
أَزَلُّ - هَزَلُّ	بَرَاءَةٌ - بَرَاعَةٌ
تَسَاءَلَ - تَسَاهَلَ	أَرْضٌ - عَرْضٌ

ث - ذ (٤)	ت - ط (٣)
نَثَرَ - نَذَرَ	تِينٌ - طِينٌ
نَفَثَ - نَفَذَ	تَيَّارٌ - طَيَّارٌ
ثَابَ - ذَابَ	تَاقَ - طَاقَ
جَثَمَ - جَذَمَ	تَابَ - طَابَ
ثِمَارٌ - ذِمَارٌ	تَرَفٌ - طَرَفٌ
ثَلَّ - ذَلَّ	ثَبَّتَ - ثَبَّطَ
بَثَّ - بَذَّ	تَمْرٌ - طَمْرٌ
ثَمَّ - ذَمَّ	تَلَا - طَلَا

86

ج - ش (٦)	ث - س (٥)
شَاءَ - جَاءَ	ثَارَ - سَارَ
شَاعَ - جَاعَ	نَثْرٌ - نَسْرٌ
شَعَلَ - جَعَلَ	ثَمِينٌ - سَمِينٌ
نَشَرَ - نَجَرَ	مَكَثَ - مَكَسَ
رَشَفَ - رَجَفَ	حَرَثَ - حَرَسَ
بُرْشٌ - بُرْجٌ	أَثَرَ - أَسَرَ
شَمَالٌ - جَمَالٌ	حَدَثٌ - حَدَسَ
خَرَشَ - خَرَجَ	إِثْمٌ - إِسْمٌ

87

ح - ع (٨)	ح - خ (٧)
بَعَثَ - بَحَثَ	نَخَبَ - نَحَبَ
شَرَعَ - شَرَحَ	نَفَخَ - نَفَحَ
جَمَعَ - جَمَحَ	خَمَلَ - حَمَلَ
لَمَعَ - لَمَحَ	خَرَقَ - حَرَقَ
نَصَعَ - نَصَحَ	خَدٌّ - حَدٌّ
مَنَعَ - مَنَحَ	خَلٌّ - حَلٌّ
سِعْرٌ - سِحْرٌ	خَسٌّ - حَسٌّ
قَمْعٌ - قَمْحٌ	صَاخِب - صَاحِبٌ

خ - غ (١٠)	ح - هـ (٩)
خَمَدَ - غَمَدَ	حَمَلَ - هَمَلَ
خَلَقَ - غَلَقَ	حَزَمَ - هَزَمَ
خَابَ - غَابَ	نَبَحَ - نَبَهَ
خَرَقَ - غَرَقَ	حَدَّدَ - هَدَّدَ
خَرَبَ - غَرَبَ	فَهْمٌ - فَحْمٌ
خَمَرَ - غَمَرَ	شَبَحٌ - شَبَهٌ
خَالٍ - غَالٍ	محْنَةٌ - مِهْنَةٌ
خِلَافٌ - غِلَافٌ	نَحْلَةٌ - نَهْلَةٌ

ذ - ز (١٢)	د - ض (١١)
عَذَلَ - عَزَلَ	دَرْبُ - ضَرْبُ
بَذَلَ - بَزَلَ	هَدَمَ - هَضَمَ
ذَرَعَ - زَرَعَ	نَقَدَ - نَقَضَ
عَذَبَ - عَزَبَ	رَدَعَ - رَضَعَ
ذُبَالَةٌ - زُبَالَةٌ	وَدَعَ - وَضَعَ
بَذَّ - بَزَّ	خَدَعَ - خَضَعَ
ذَلَّ - زَلَّ	نَهَدَ - نَهَضَ
ذَمَّ - زَمَّ	قِرْدُ - قِرْضُ

ر – غ (١٤)	ذ – ظ (١٣)
صَبَرَ – صَبَغَ	نَذَرَ – نَظَرَ
رَبَطَ – غَبَطَ	ذَلَّ – ظَلَّ
رَمَقَ – غَمَقَ	فَذُّ – فَظُّ
صَارَ – صَاغَ	عَذَلَ – عَاظَلَ
زَارَ – زَاغَ	حَاذَرَ – حَظَرَ
رَمَزَ – غَمَزَ	ذَرْفٌ – ظَرْفٌ
رَمَى – غَمَى	بَذَّ – بَظَّ
بَرَى – بَغَى	دَفَرُ – ظَفَرُ

ز - س (١٦)	ر - ل (١٥)
زَارَ - سَارَ	سَارَ - سَالَ
رَزَمَ - رَسَمَ	زَارَ - زَالَ
غَزَلَ - غَسَلَ	مَرَّ - مَلَّ
غَمَزَ - غَمَسَ	سَاحِرٌ - سَاحِلٌ
نَزَلَ - نَسَلَ	بَصَرٌ - بَصَلٌ
نَزَفَ - نَسَفَ	جِدَارٌ - جِدَالٌ
حَزَمَ - حَسَمَ	تَكَرَّمَ - تَكَلَّمَ
زَاغَ - سَاغَ	اِسْتِقْرَارُ - اِسْتِقْلَالُ

ض - ظ (١٨)	س - ص (١٧)
حَضَرَ - حَظَرَ	سَارَ - صَارَ
نَضَرَ - نَظَرَ	نَسْرُ - نَصْرُ
حَضَّ - حَظَّ	سَبَحَ - صَبَحَ
قَرَّضَ - قَرَّظَ	فَسِيحٌ - فَصِيحٌ
ضَنَّ - ظَنَّ	سَيْفٌ - صَيْفٌ
ضَلَّ - ظَلَّ	قَسْرُ - قَصْرُ
فَضٌّ - فَظٌّ	سَلَبَ - صَلَبَ
ضَهْرُ - ظَهْرُ	سَدَّ - صَدَّ

93

غ - ق (٢٠)	ع - غ (١٩)
غَلَى - قَلَى	بَلَعَ - بَلَغَ
غَلَبَ - قَلَبَ	شَعَلَ - شَغَلَ
غَا مَرَ - قَا مَرَ	طَعَامٌ - طَغَامٌ
غَرِيبٌ - قَرِيبٌ	شَعْبٌ - شَغْبٌ
فَرَغَ - فَرَقَ	عَزَلَ - غَزَلَ
فَغَرَ - فَقَرَ	عَابَ - غَابَ
أَلْغَى - أَلْقَى	نَبَعَ - نَبَغَ
نَغَّصَ - نَقَّصَ	شَاعِرٌ - شَاغِرٌ

94

ق - ك (٢٢)	ع - هـ (٢١)
قَلْبٌ - كَلْبٌ	عَابَ - هَابَ
رَقَدَ - رَكَدَ	شَعْرُ - شَهْرُ
قَادَ - كَادَ	جِعَةٌ - جِهَةٌ
نَهِيقٌ - نَهِيك	نَبَعَ - نَبَهَ
رَقِيقٌ - ركِيكٌ	أَعَانَ - أَهَانَ
سَبَقَ - سَبَكَ	عَامٌّ - هَامٌّ
قَرَّرَ - كَرَّرَ	عَوَى - هَوَى
قُلْ - كُلْ	عَرَّبَ - هَرَّبَ

95

Word-pairs
distinguished by lengthening and stressing

أزواج الكلمات

مميزة حسب

المد والتشديد

سَعِيدٌ	–	سَاعِدٌ	أُذُنٌ – أُذُونٌ
سَفِيرٌ	–	سَافِرٌ	بَارِدٌ – بَرِيدٌ
شَعِيرٌ	–	شَاعِرٌ	بَالِغٌ – بَلِيغٌ
طَلَى	–	طَالَ	بَانَ – بَنَى
طَوِيلَةٌ	–	طَاوِلَةٌ	ثَامِنٌ – ثَمِينٌ
عَدِيلٌ	–	عَادِلٌ	جَمَلٌ – جَمَالٌ
عَارَضَ	–	عَرَضَ	حَادِثٌ – حَدِيثٌ
عَاكَسَ	–	عَكَسَ	دَانَ – دَنَى
قَدِيمٌ	–	قَادِمٌ	ذَهَبُ – ذَهَابٌ
قَرِيبٌ	–	قَارِبٌ	رَابِعٌ – رَبِيعٌ

نَظِيرٌ	نَاظِرٌ -	وَاصَلَ	وَصَلَ -
فَرِيقٌ	فَارِقٌ -	قَدَّمَ	قَدِمَ -
بَشَّرَ	بَاشَرَ -	قَبَّلَ	قَابَلَ -
مَدَّ	مَدَى -	فَرَّ	فَارَ -
مَلَّ	مَالَ -	كَاتَبَ	كَتَبَ -
مَثَّلَ	مَاثَلَ -	كَتِيبَةٌ	كَاتِبَةٌ -
كَفَّ	كَفَى -	كَمِينٌ	كَامِنٌ -
عَبَّرَ	عَبَرَ -	كَتَبْنَا	كَتَبْنَ -
شَكَّ	شَكَا -	مَتَى	مَاتَ -
سَمَّى	سَمَا -	مَطَارٌ	مَطَرٌ -

99

أَعَدَّ - أَعَادَ	رَبَّى - رَبَّى	
أَمُرُّ - آمُرُ	رَشَّ - رَشَا	
أَمَّنَ - آمَنَ	خَالٌ - خَلٌّ	
جَدٌّ - جَادٌّ	حَوَّلَ - حَاوَلَ	
بَلَّغَ - بَالَغَ - بَلَغَ	حَمَّامٌ - حَمَامٌ	
صَدَّرَ - صَادَرَ - صَدَرَ	حَادٌّ - حَدٌّ	
نَامَ - نَمَا - نَمَّ - نَمَى	هَامٌّ - هَمٌّ	
قَالَ - قَلَى - قَلَّ	هُنَّ - هُنَا	
عَدَا - عَادَ - عَدَّ	اِسْتَعَدَّ - اِسْتَعَادَ	
عَامٌ - عَامٌّ - عَمَّ	اِسْتَقَلَّ - اِسْتَقَالَ	

100

List of the words cited in the Handbook

قائمة بالمفردات الواردة في الكتاب

rice	أَرُزٌّ	pits, pl.	آبَارُ
earth	أَرْضُ	traces, vestige	آثَارُ
eternity	أَزَلُ	baked bricks	آجُرُّ
to capture	أَسَرَ	other	آخَرُ
cement	أَسْمَنْتُ	Adam	آدَمُ
markets	أَسْوَاقٌ	May	آذَارُ
to repeat	أَعَادَ	Arameans	الْآرَامِيُّونَ
to help	أَعَانَ	sorry	آسِفٌ
to prepare	أَعَدَّ	to console, comfort	آسَى
feasts	أَعْيَادٌ	machine	آلَةُ
elephants	أَفْيَالٌ	hopes	آمَالُ
to eat	أَكَلَ	I command	آمُرُ
to annul, abrogate	أَلْغَى	to believe	آمَنَ
to throw	أَلْقَى	now	الْآنَ
pain	أَلَمُّ	Miss	آنِسَةُ
mother	أُمُّ	father	أَبُ
I go by	أَمُرُّ	to report, relate	أَثَرَ
hope, n.	أَمَلٌ	generations	أَجْيَالٌ
to hope	أَمَلَ	to educate, punish	أَدَّبَ
to assure, endure	أَمَّنَ	ear	أُذُنُ
miles	أَمْيَالٌ	permissions	أُذُونُ

102

to undertake	بَاشَرَ	admiral	أَمِيرُ الْبَحْرِ
to sell	بَاعَ	to humiliate	أَهَانَ
mind	بَالٌ	orchestra	أُورِكِسْتْرَا
to exaggerate	بَالَغَ	to seek refuge	أَوَى
mature, of age	بَالِغٌ	sin, offense, rime	إِثْمٌ
to be clear	بَانَ	noun, name	إِسْمٌ
petroleum	بِتْرُولٌ	except	إِلَّا
to search	بَحَثَ	prayer leader	إِمَامٌ
to start	بَدَأَ	woman	إِمْرَأَةٌ
to seam	بَدَا	to recuperate, get back	اِسْتَعَادَ
to originate	بَدَعَ	to get ready	اِسْتَعَدَّ
to befall unexpectedly	بَدَهَ	to resign	اِسْتَقَالَ
to surpass s. o.	بَذَّ	stability	اِسْتَقْرَارُ
to give generously	بَذَلَ	to be independent	اِسْتَقَلَّ
innocence	بَرَاءَةٌ	independence	اِسْتِقْلَالٌ
efficiency	بَرَاعَةٌ	read (imperative)	اِقْرَأَ
oranges	بُرْتْقَالٌ	focus, centre	بُؤْرَةٌ
tower	بُرْجٌ	pit	بِئْرٌ
cold, n.	بَرْدٌ	door	بَابٌ
mat	بُرْشٌ	to pass, spend the night	بَاتَ
parliament	بَرْلَمَانٌ	cold, adj.	بَارِدٌ

to follow	تَبِعَ	mail, post	بَرِيدٌ
to leave	تَرَكَ	to bud, burgeon	بَزَّ
to ask o.s	تَسَاءَلَ	to split	بَزَلَ
to be indulgent	تَسَاهَلَ	to announce (as good news)	بَشَّرَ
to learn	تَعَلَّمَ	sight	بَصَرٌ
optimism	تَفَاؤُلٌ	onions	بَصَلٌ
to accept, receive	تَقَبَّلَ	slow	بَطِيءٌ
to be so kind	تَكَرَّمَ	to send	بَعَثَ
to speak	تَكَلَّمَ	to swallow	بَلَعَ
technology	تِكْنُولُوجِيا	to reach	بَلَغَ
television	تِلْفِزْيُونٌ	to convey	بَلَّغَ
telephone	تِلْفُونٌ	eloquent	بَلِيغٌ
dates	تَمَرٌ	girl	بِنْتٌ
discrimination	تَمْيِيزٌ	bank	بَنْكٌ
mulberry	تُوتٌ	to build	بَنَى
flow, stream	تَيَّارٌ	hall	بَهْوٌ
figs	تِينٌ	environment	بِيئَةٌ
to avenge	ثَأَرَ	piano	بِيَانُو
to return	ثَابَ	bureaucracy	بِيرُوقْرَاطِيَا
to revolt	ثَارَ	biology	بِيُولُوجِيَا
eighth	ثَامِنٌ	to suffer	تَأَلَّمَ

to sit down	جَلَسَ	to tear down, destroy	ثَلَّ
beauty	جَمَالٌ	snow	ثَلْجٌ
to be refractory, recalcitrant	جَمَحَ	there	ثَمَّ
to add	جَمَعَ	fruit	ثِمَارُ
camel	جَمَلٌ	precious	ثَمِينٌ
direction	جِهَةٌ	dress	ثَوْبٌ
generation	جِيلٌ	to come	جَاءَ
sharp	حَادٌّ	serious	جَادٌّ
to watch out, be careful	حَاذَرَ	neighbor	جَارٌ
condition	حَالٌ	be hungry	جَاعَ
to try	حَاوَلَ	algebra	جَبْرٌ
limit	حَدٌّ	mountain	جَبَلٌ
to limit	حَدَّ	to lie face down	جَثَمَ
event	حَدَثٌ	grandfather	جَدٌّ
to happen	حَدَثَ	wall	جِدَارٌ
to fix	حَدَّدَ	discussion	جِدَالٌ
modern, conversation	حَدِيثٌ	to cut off	جَذَمَ
to plough	حَرَثَ	part	جُزْءٌ
to watch, guard	حَرَسَ	beer	جِعَةٌ
to burn	حَرَقَ	to put, place, lay	جَعَلَ
to tie up	حَزَمَ	geography	جُغْرَافِيَا

105

autumn, fall	خَرِيفٌ	to feel (action)	حَسَّ
lettuce	خَسٌّ	to decide	حَسَمَ
to submit	خَضَعَ	to incite	حَضَّ
vinegar	خَلٌّ	to attend	حَضَرَ
conflict	خِلَافٌ	to be lucky	حَظَّ
to create	خَلَقَ	to prohibit	حَظَرَ
to calm down	خَمَدَ	to preserve, guard	حفظ
to cover	خَمَرَ	milk	حَلِيبٌ
to be weak	خَمَلَ	pigeon	حَمَامٌ
always	دَائِماً	bath	حَمَّامٌ
to be dizzy	دَاخَ	to carry	حَمَلَ
house, habitation	دَارٌ	to transform	حَوَّلَ
to turn	دَارَ	to fail	خَابَ
to owe	دَانَ	maternal uncle	خَالٌ
to enter	دَخَلَ	empty	خَالٍ
path, road	دَرْبٌ	news	خَبَرٌ
lesson	دَرْسٌ	cheek	خَدٌّ
stench	دَفَرٌ	to cheat	خَدَعَ
doctor	دُكْتُورٌ	to go out	خَرَجَ
democracy	دِمُقْرَاطِيَةٌ	to scratch	خَرَشَ
to approach	دَنَا	to pierce	خَرَقَ

quarter	رُبْعٌ	houses, habitations	دُورٌ
living zones	رُبُوعٌ	religion	دِينٌ
to raise, educate	رَبَّى	register, cabinet	دِيوَانٌ
spring	رَبِيعٌ	to melt	ذَابَ
to return	رَجَعَ	wick	ذُبَالَةٌ
man	رَجُلٌ	to measure	ذَرَعَ
to send back, to return	رَدَّ	to flow, shed (tears), action	ذَرْفٌ
to repel	رَدَعَ	to be low, lowly	ذَلَّ
to bundle	رَزَمَ	to blame	ذَمَّ
to draw	رَسَمَ	sacred possession	ذِمَارٌ
to spatter	رَشَّ	to go, v.n.	ذَهَابٌ
to bribe	رَشَا	old	ذَهَبٌ
to suck, sip	رَشَفَ	to go	ذَهَبَ
to refuse	رَفَضَ	taste	ذَوْقٌ
to raise	رَفَعَ	presidency	رِئَاسَةٌ
to lie down	رَقَدَ	president	رَئِيسٌ
thin, slender	رَقِيقٌ	fourth	رَابِعٌ
to be stagnant	رَكَدَ	radio	رَادِيو
pitiful, weak	رَكِيكٌ	to plead	رَافَعَ
to make a sign	رَمَزَ	to grow	رَبَا
to glance	رَمَقَ	to tie	رَبَطَ

107

to travel	سَافَرَ	to throw, cast	رَمَى
unveiled	سَافِرٌ	soul	رُوحٌ
to flow, stream	سَالَ	wind	رِيحٌ
to swim	سَبَحَ	to roar	زَأَرَ
to recede	سَبَقَ	to visit	زَارَ
to found (metal)	سَبَكَ	to deviate	زَاغَ
to record	سَجَّلَ	to disappear	زَالَ
magic	سِحْرٌ	rubbish	زُبَالَةٌ
to plug up	سَدَّ	to sow	زَرَعَ
price	سِعْرٌ	to slip	زَلَّ
to cough	سَعَلَ	to glide	زَلَقَ
happy	سَعِيدٌ	tie up, fasten	زَمَّ
to remove a veil	سَفَرَ	colleague	زَمِيلٌ
ambassador	سَفِيرٌ	to shine	زَهَرَ
to fall	سَقَطَ	to ask	سَأَلَ
sugar	سُكَّرٌ	question	سُؤَالٌ
to inhabit	سَكَّنَ	magician	سَاحِرٌ
peace	سَلَامٌ	coast	سَاحِلٌ
to take away	سَلَبَ	to walk	سَارَ
to be high	سَمَا	forearm	سَاعِدٌ
to hear	سَمِعَ	to be easy to swallow	سَاغَ

people	شَعْبُ	symphony	سِمْفُونِيَةُ
hair	شَعْرُ	fish	سَمَكُ
to inflame	شَعَلَ	to name	سَمَّى
barley	شَعِيرُ	fat	سَمِينُ
unrest	شَغَبُ	year	سَنَةُ
to occupy	شَغَلَ	market	سُوقُ
to doubt	شَكَّ	walk, march	سَيْرُ
to complain	شَكَا	conduct	سِيرَةُ
thanks	شُكْرَاً	sword	سَيْفُ
to smell	شَمَّ	senator	سِينَاتُورُ
north	شَمَالُ	to want	شَاءَ
sun	شَمْسُ	poet	شَاعِرُ
month	شَهْرُ	empty	شَاغِرُ
thing	شَيْءُ	tea	شَايُ
to shout	صَاحَ	ghost	شَبَحُ
friend	صَاحِبُ	resemblance	شَبَهُ
noisy	صَاخِبُ	to make firm, tighten	شَدَّ
to seize	صَادَرَ	to intensify	شَدَّدَ
to become	صَارَ	to drink	شَرِبَ
to shape	صَاغَ	condition	شَرْطُ
to pour	صَبَّ	to begin	شَرَعَ

109

table	طَاوِلَةٌ	to beam	صَبَّحَ
peacock	طَاوُوسٌ	to be patient	صَبَرَ
food	طَعَامٌ	to dye	صَبَغَ
populace	طَغَامٌ	to turn away	صَدَّ
to ask	طَلَبَ	to be issued	صَدَرَ
to paint	طَلَى	to export	صَدَّرَ
tomatoes	طَمَاطِمُ	friend	صَدِيقٌ
length	طُولٌ	to go up	صَعِدَ
long, f.	طَوِيلَةٌ	zero	صِفْرٌ
pilot	طَيَّارٌ	to crucify	صَلَبَ
clay	طِينٌ	voice	صَوْتٌ
charm, envelope	ظَرْفٌ	summer	صَيْفٌ
victory	ظَفَرٌ	to beat	ضَرَبَ
nail, claw	ظُفْرٌ	to beat, v.n.	ضَرْبٌ
to remain	ظَلَّ	to go astray	ضَلَّ
darkness	ظَلَامٌ	to be stingy	ضَنَّ
to think	ظَنَّ	top of a mountain	ضَهْرٌ
back	ظَهْرٌ	guest	ضَيْفٌ
to appear	ظَهَرَ	to be able	طَاقَ
to reprove	عَابَ	to be long	طَالَ
to return	عَادَ	student	طَالِبٌ

110

to isolate	عَزَلَ	to be equal	عَادَلَ
to prevent	عَضَلَ	just	عَادِلٌ
to be thirsty	عَطِشَ	to take refuge	عَاذَ
I beg your pardon!	عَفْواً	to oppose	عَارَضَ
to reflect	عَكَسَ	to be repetitious	عَاظَلَ
to be high	عَلَا	to contradict	عَاكَسَ
flag	عَلَمٌ	world	عَالَمٌ
to teach	عَلَّمَ	year	عَامٌ
paternal uncle	عَمٌّ	general, adj.	عَامٌّ
to be populated	عَمَرَ	to cross	عَبَرَ
work, n.	عَمَلٌ	to express	عَبَّرَ
agent	عَمِيلٌ	to count	عَدَّ
stick	عُودٌ	to run	عَدَا
to howl (wolf)	عَوَى	to act justly	عَدَلَ
feast	عِيدٌ	equal	عَدِيلٌ
eye	عَيْنٌ	to hinder	عَذَبَ
to be absent	غَابَ	to rebuke	عَذَلَ
to anger	غَاظَ	width	عَرْضٌ
expensive	غَالٍ	to exhibit	عَرَضَ
to venture, to risk	غَامَرَ	to know	عَرَفَ
to envy	غَبَطَ	to be far	عَزَبَ

111

distinctive, differential	فَارِقٌ	gram	غِرَامٌ
to overflow	فَاضَ	to set (sun)	غَرَبَ
young woman	فَتَاةٌ	west	غَرْبٌ
to open	فَتَحَ	to plant	غَرَسَ
to examine	فَحَصَ	to be drowned	غَرِقَ
coal	فَحْمٌ	strange, foreign	غَرِيبٌ
glory, honour	فَخْرٌ	to spin	غَزَلَ
unusual	فَذٌّ	to wash	غَسَلَ
to run away	فَرَّ	envelope	غِلَافٌ
to sort	فَرَزَ	to subdue, conquer	غَلَبَ
to spread	فَرَشَ	to close, shut	غَلَقَ (أَغْلَقَ)
to be empty	فَرَغَ	to boil	غَلَى
to distinguish, to separate	فَرَقَ	to sheathe	غَمَدَ
fur(s)	فَرْوٌ	to inundate, overflow	غَمَرَ
team	فَرِيقٌ	to make a sign	غَمَزَ
spacious	فَسِيحٌ	to dip	غَمَسَ
to separate	فَصَلَ	to be dump	غَمَقَ
class, chapter	فَصْلٌ	to roof (a house)	غَمَى
eloquent	فَصِيحٌ	mouse, rat	فَأْرٌ
dispersion	فَضٌّ	group, class	فِئَةٌ
to prefer	فَضَّلَ	to boil	فَارَ

112

captain	قُبْطَانٌ	favor, benefit	فَضْلٌ
to kiss	قَبَّلَ	crude	فَظٌّ
foot	قَدَمٌ	to open (the mouth) wide	فَغَرَ
to precede	قَدَمَ	to pierce	فَقَرَ
to present, introduce	قَدَّمَ	mouth	فَمٌ
old, ancient	قَدِيمٌ	to understand	فَهَمَ
Koran	اَلْقُرْآنُ	comprehension	فَهَّمٌ
to read	قَرَأَ	phosphate	فُوسْفَاتٌ
ape	قِرْدٌ	towels, napkins pl.	فُوَطٌ
to decide	قَرَّرَ	towel, napkin	فُوطَةٌ
to pinch	قَرَصَ	beans	فُولٌ
disk	قُرْصٌ	physics	فِيزِيَا
to gnaw, chew up	قَرَّضَ	elephant	فِيلٌ
credit	قَرْضٌ	philosopher	فَيْلَسُوفٌ
to praise	قَرَّظَ	to meet	قَابَلَ
century	قَرْنٌ	to lead	قَادَ
near, close	قَرِيبٌ	coming, next	قَادِمٌ
coercion	قَسْرٌ	boat	قَارِبٌ
to divide, distribute	قَسَّمَ	judge	قَاضٍ
castle	قَصْرٌ	to say, tell	قَالَ
to jump	قَفَزَ	to gamble, hazard	قَامَرَ

to write	كَتَبَ	to decrease	قَلَّ
they (f.pl.) wrote	كَتَبْنَ	say (imperative)	قُلْ
we wrote	كَتَبْنَا	to turn around	قَلَبَ
alcohol	كُحُولٌ	heart	قَلْبٌ
to repeat	كَرَّرَ	pen, pencil	قَلَمٌ
chair	كُرْسِيٌّ	to fry	قَلَى
to disclose	كَشَفَ	wheat	قَمْحٌ
to desist	كَفَّ	moon	قَمَرٌ
to sponsor	كَفَلَ	repression	قَمْعٌ
to suffice	كَفَى	consul	قُنْصُلٌ
eat (imperative)	كُلْ	nutriment, food	قُوتٌ
dog	كَلْبٌ	guitar	قيثَارَةٌ
ambush	كَمِينٌ	values	قِيَمٌ
be (imperative)	كُنْ	value	قيمَةٌ
drinking glass	كُوبٌ	to correspond	كَاتَبَ
bag, purse	كِيسٌ	to be on the point of	كَادَ
how	كَيْفَ	caricature	كَارِيكَاتُورِيٌّ
kilogram	كِيلُوغرامٌ	sufficient, enough	كَافٍ
kilometer	كِيلُومتْرٌ	hidden	كَامِنٌ
chemistry	كيمِيَا	to enlarge	كَبَّرَ
necessary, obligatory	لَازِمٌ	book	كِتَابٌ

to expand, to extend	مَدَّدَ	to put on, wear (clothes)	لَبِسَ
range, scope	مَدَى	liter, litre	لِتْرٌ
city	مَدِينَةٌ	refuge	لُجُوءٌ
to go by, pass	مَرَّ	to play	لَعِبَ
mirror	مِرْآةٌ	to glance	لَمَحَ
welcome!	مَرْحَباً	to gleam	لَمَعَ
to fall ill, sick	مَرِضَ	night	لَيْلٌ
flexible	مَرِنٌ	shelter, place of refuge	مَأْوَى
to tear	مَزَّقَ	water	مَاءٌ
to touch	مَسَّ	to die	مَاتَ
question	مَسْأَلَةٌ	to resemble	مَاثَلَ
airport	مَطَارٌ	machine	مَاكِينَةٌ
rain	مَطَرٌ	meter	مِتْرٌ
to remain	مَكَثَ	when (interrogative)	مَتَى
to collect taxes	مَكَسَ	example, proverb	مَثَلٌ
to be bored	مَلَّ	to represent	مَثَّلَ
who (interrogative)	مَنْ	lawyer	مُحَامٍ
to grant	مَنَحَ	affliction, hardship	مِحْنَةٌ
to prevent	مَنَعَ	storehouse, storage room	مَخْزِنٌ
profession	مِهْنَةٌ	to be mistaken, wrong	مُخْطِئٌ
stuff, matter, materials	مَوَادٌّ	to extend	مَدَّ

to exhaust	نَزَفَ	bananas	مَوْزٌ
to go down	نَزَلَ	mile	مِيلٌ
to weave	نَسَجَ	to sleep	نَامَ
vulture	نَسْرٌ	fire	نَارٌ
to blow up	نَسَفَ	to be hostile, fight	نَاصَبَ
to pluck out	نَسَلَ	look, glance	نَاظِرٌ
to forget	نَسِيَ	news	نَبَأٌ
to publish	نَشَرَ	to inform	نَبَّأَ
to raise, rear, erect	نَصَبَ	to bark	نَبَحَ
to give advice	نَصَحَ	to well	نَبَعَ
victory	نَصْرٌ	to emerge	نَبَغَ
to be clear	نَصَعَ	to be well-know	نَبُهَ
to be bright	نَضَرَ	to warn	نَبَّهَ
to pronounce	نَطَقَ	to scatter	نَثَرَ
to look	نَظَرَ	prose	نَثْرٌ
counterpart	نَظِيرٌ	to be successful	نَجَحَ
yes	نَعَمْ	to hew, carve, plane (wood)	نَجَرَ
to disturb, ruffle, spoil	نَغَّصَ	to lament	نَحَبَ
to cough out	نَفَثَ	bee	نَحْلَةٌ
to blow	نَفَحَ	to select	نَخَبَ
to be used up	نَفَدَ	to consecrate	نَذَرَ

to threaten	هَدَّد	to pierce	نَفَذَ
to demolish	هَدَم	to pay in cash, to peck	نَقَدَ
quiet(ness)	هُدُوءٌ	to carve out	نَقَشَ
to help to escape	هَرَّب	to decrease	نَقَصَ
to flee	هَرَب	to tear down, to abrogate	نَقَضَ
to be emaciated, to joke	هَزَلٌ	to transport	نَقَلَ
to defeat	هَزَم	pure, clean	نَقِيٌّ
to digest	هَضَم	to reveal	نَمَّ
worry, anxiety	هَمٌّ	to grow, increase	نَمَا
to shed tears	هَمَل	to promote	نَمَّى
they, f.pl.	هُنَّ	to become round	نَهَدَ
here	هُنَا	to rise	نَهَضَ
air	هَوَاءٌ	gulp, draught	نَهْلَةٌ
to tumble	هَوَى	braying	نَهِيقٌ
to prepare, to make ready	هَيَّأَ	exhausted	نَهِيكٌ
to continue	وَاصَل	light	نُورٌ
to find	وَجَدَ	to intend	نَوَى
face	وَجْهٌ	yoke	نِيرٌ
to love, like (would like)	وَدَّ	to fear	هَابَ
to let, leave	وَدَع	important	هَامٌّ
to bid farewell	وَدَّع	to fringe	هَدَّبَ

to arrive	وَصَلَ
to put	وَضَعَ
boy	وَلَدٌ
to dry	يَبِسَ
hand	يَدٌ
day	يَوْمٌ

List of the cities and countries cited in the Handbook

قائمة بأسماء البلدان والمدن الواردة في الكتاب

Morocco	اَلْمَغْرِبُ	Azerbaijan	آذَرْبَيْجَانُ
India	اَلْهِنْدُ	Asia	آسِيَا
Paris	بَارِيسُ	Abu Dhabi	أَبُوظَبِي
Pakistan	بَاكِسْتَانُ	Athens	أَثِينَا
Baghdad	بَغْدَادُ	Germany	أَلْمَانِيَا
Bonn	بُونْ	America	أَمريكَا
Bethlehem	بَيْتَ لَحْمُ	Europe	أُورُوبَا
Beirut	بَيْرُوتُ	Africa	إِفْرِيقِيَا
Turkey	تُرْكِيَا	Italy	إِيطَالِيَا
Tunisia	تُونِسُ	Jordan	اَلأُرْدُنُ
Jeddah	جَدَّةُ	Algeria	اَلْجَزَائِرُ
Geneva	جِنِيفْ	Khartoum	اَلْخُرْطُومُ
Damascus	دِمَشْقُ	Riyadh	اَلرِّيَاضُ
Russia	رُوسِيَا	Senegal	اَلسِّنِغَالُ
Rome	رُومَا	Sudan	اَلسُّودَانُ
Syria	سُورِيَا	Iraq	اَلْعِرَاقُ
Sanaa	صَنْعَاءُ	Cairo	اَلْقَاهِرَةُ
Teheran	طَهْرَانُ	Kuwait	اَلْكُوَيْتُ

Amman	عَمَّانُ
Oman	عُمَانُ
France	فَرَنْسَا
Qatar	قَطَرُ
Canada	كَنَدَا
The Hague	لَاهَايْ
Lebanon	لُبْنَانُ
London	لَنْدَنُ
Libya	لِيبِيَا
Malaysia	مَالِيزيَا
Madrid	مَدْرِيدُ
Egypt	مِصْرُ